AF584646

The Berenstain Bears'®

Country Cookbook

Cub-Friendly Cooking with an Adult

ZONDERKIDZ

Requests for information should be addressed to:
Zonderkidz, 3900 *Sparks Dr. SE, Grand Rapids, Michigan 49546*

ISBN 978-0-310-74720-8

Editor: Mary Hassinger
Design: Cindy Davis

Printed in China

14 15 16 17 18 19 /DSC/ 10 9 8 7 6 5 4 3 2 1

By Mike Berenstain
Based on the characters created by
Stan & Jan Berenstain

Contents

Breakfast....page 4

Lunch....page 26

Main Dishes....page 48

Dessert & Snacks....page 70

Mama Bear was always telling the cubs, "Breakfast is a very important meal."

She knew if her cubs started their day with a healthy breakfast they would have plenty of energy for a busy morning of school, baseball, soccer, or whatever they were up to that day.

"What are the best foods to eat for breakfast, Mama?" Sister Bear asked one day.

"Let's head to the kitchen, cubs! We can look through my cookbooks and find some recipes. Then we'll cook up a healthy breakfast for all of us to enjoy," Mama said as she, Brother, Sister, and Honey Bear headed for the kitchen.

This was a great way to start the day ... working together to make a delicious meal to share.

Breakfast

Bear-y Delicious Scones

What you need:

Scones:

- 1 box scone mix (or your favorite recipe)
- 1 cup fresh or frozen blueberries
- 2 tablespoons chocolate chips

Glaze:

- 1 cup powdered sugar
- 1–2 tablespoons milk
- 1 tablespoon soft butter
- 1/2 teaspoon vanilla or lemon flavoring

Directions

1. Mix scones according to package directions.
2. Add blueberries, and mix in gently.
3. Roll scone dough 1/2–inch thick. Cut into 12 circles with a 2–inch cookie cutter.
4. Place 8 of the scones on an ungreased baking sheet to make teddy bear heads.
5. Cut the other four scones into four pie–shaped pieces each to make teddy bear ears.
6. Attach two pieces on each and shape to look like rounded ears.
7. Bake according to package directions.
8. While scones bake, combine glaze ingredients and mix with spoon.
9. Remove baked scones from oven and cool slightly.
10. While still warm, frost scones with a thin layer of glaze. Add chocolate chips to each scone for eyes and a nose.
11. Serve with butter and honey.

Yield: 8 scones

Bunny Biscuits

What you need:

- 1 tube (7–1/2 oz.) refrigerated buttermilk biscuits
- 10 choclate chips
- 5 raisins
- 20 slivered almonds

Directions

1. Gently shape five biscuits into oval shapes; place on a greased baking sheet about 2 inches apart. Cut remaining biscuits in half. Shape biscuit halves to form ears; press firmly to attach to whole biscuits. On each biscuit, press on two chocolate chip eyes, one raisin nose, and four slivered almond whiskers.
2. Bake at 375 degrees for 8–10 minutes or until biscuits are browned. Cool slightly.

Yield: 5 servings

Serve with honey for a sweet treat.

Bear-y Good Oatmeal

What you need:

- 2 cups water
- 2/3 cup old-fashioned oatmeal
- 1/4 teaspoon nutmeg
- 1/2 teaspoon cinnamon
- 1–2 tablespoons honey
- 1/2 cup almond milk (or regular milk)
- 1 peach, peeled and cut in thin slices
- Nutmeg and cinnamon to sprinkle on top

Directions

1. Boil water, then stir in oatmeal, nutmeg, and cinnamon. Boil about two minutes.
2. Turn down the heat and let simmer a coup more minutes, until it reaches the desired consistency.
3. Remove from heat. Divide into 2 bowls and add milk.
4. Top with peaches and honey and sprinkle with cinnamon and nutmeg.

Yield: 2 servings

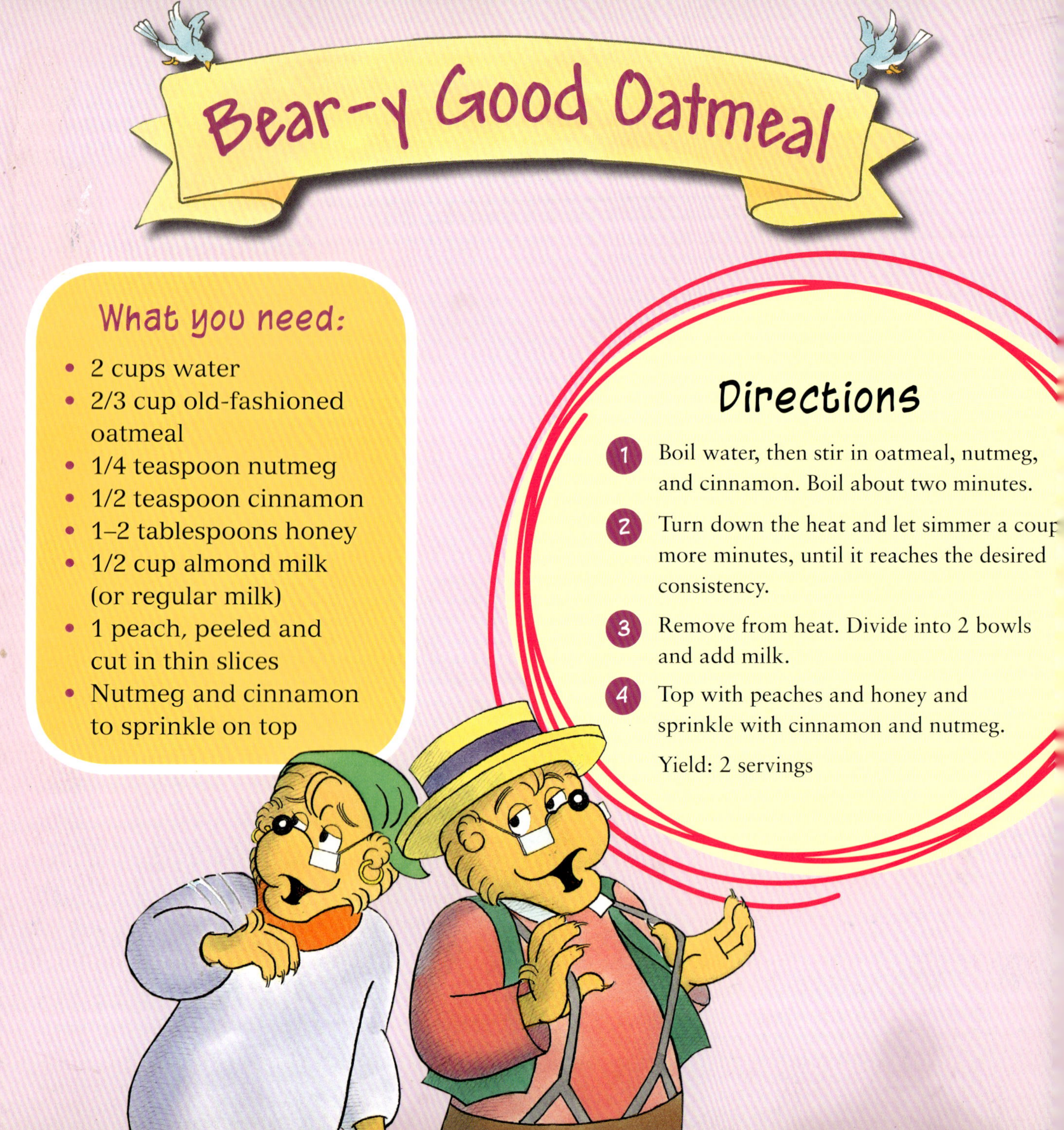

What you need:

- 1 cup all-purpose flour
- 2 eggs
- 1/2 cup milk
- 1/2 cup water
- 1/4 teaspoon salt
- 2 tablespoons butter, melted
- Strawberries and blueberries, optional

Directions

1. In a large mixing bowl, whisk together the flour and the eggs. Gradually add the milk and water, stirring to combine. Add the salt and butter; beat until smooth.
2. Heat a lightly oiled griddle or frying pan over medium high heat. Pour or scoop 1/4 cup of the batter onto the griddle. Tilt the pan with a circular motion so that the batter coats the surface evenly.
3. Cook the crepe for about 2 minutes, until the bottom is light brown. Loosen with a spatula, turn, and cook the other side. Serve hot.
4. You can fill with whipped cream or custard. Also, top with berries for a healthy breakfast.

Yield: 8 crepes

For an even sweeter treat, drizzle crepes with honey.

Tasty Toboggans

What you need:

- 3–4 eggs
- 1/4 cup milk
- 4 slices bread
- 6–8 strips fried bacon or cooked links of sausage
- Butter and syrup

Directions

1. Beat eggs and stir in milk. Dip both sides of bread slices into egg mixture.
2. Brown bread slices on a greased skillet to make French toast.
3. Place two bacon strips or sausage "runners" side by side on a plate.
4. Top with one slice of warm French toast to make a toboggan.
5. Sprinkle with powdered sugar for snow.
6. Serve with butter and syrup.

Try using honey instead of syrup.

Fruit Salad

What you need:

- 3 cups cubed seedless watermelon
- 1 fresh pineapple, peeled, cored, and cut into 1–inch chunks
- 1 pound fresh strawberries, hulled and quartered
- 3 cups seedless grapes
- 3 cups cubed cantaloupe

Directions

1. Toss all the fruit into a bowl. Mix well.
2. Chill the fruit salad until ready to serve.

Yield: about 15 cups

Top with fresh lime juice and honey for a sweeter treat.

Monkey Bread

What you need:

- 1 cup sugar
- 1 tablespoon cinnamon
- 2 (6.3 oz.) cans of refrigerated biscuits
- 1/2 cup butter
- 1/2 cup brown sugar
- 2 tablespoons honey

Directions

1. Preheat oven to 350 degrees. Grease bundt pan well, and set aside.
2. Combine cinnamon and sugar in a large zip–closed bag.
3. Separate the biscuits. Cut each into 4 pieces. Place about half of them into the bag. Shake to coat the pieces.
4. Place the biscuits into the bundt pan. Place the remaining biscuits into the bag and repeat coating. Place all of the dough in the pan.
5. In a small bowl, microwave the butter, brown sugar, and honey. Pour over the biscuits in the pan.
6. Bake 28–32 minutes. Cool in the pan for about 10 minutes.
7. Turn upside down onto a serving plate and serve warm.

Yield: about 15 servings

Sausage & Tater Tots Wraps

What you need:

- 2 sausage patties
- 9 tater tots
- 2 tablespoons ketchup
- 1 slice American cheese
- 1 whole wheat tortilla

Directions

1. Prepare sausage as directed.
2. Prepare tater tots as directed.
3. Squirt ketchup onto whole wheat wrap. Top with warm sausage, tater tots, and cheese.
4. Roll it up and enjoy!

Yield: 1 serving

Scotch Eggs

What you need:

- 5 eggs
- 1 pound ground breakfast sausage
- 1/2 cup all-purpose flour
- 2 cups dry bread crumbs

Directions

1. Place five eggs in a single layer in a saucepan.
2. Cover eggs with cold water so that water is an inch or two above egg
3. Put saucepan on stove on high heat and bring water to a boil.
4. As soon as water begins to boil, reduce heat to low.
5. Let simmer for one minute, then remove pan from heat.
6. Cover saucepan and let sit for 12 minutes.
7. Remove eggs from water and let cool.
8. When eggs are cool, remove shells.
9. Evenly divide breakfast sausage into 5 portions.
10. Roll an egg in flour.
11. Evenly wrap one portion of sausage around floured egg, ensuring that egg is covered completely.
12. Roll egg/sausage ball in bread crumbs.
13. Repeat with remaining eggs and sausage.
14. Bake at 375 degrees for 30 minutes or until bread crumbs are golden-brown.

Yield: 5 eggs

Toast with Eggs & Cheese

What you need:

- 4 slices bread
- 4 eggs
- 4 sausage patties (optional)
- 4 slices American or Cheddar cheese

Directions

1. Toast and butter bread. Using a round cookie cutter or drinking glass, cut a circle out of each toast slice and set aside.
2. Scramble eggs and cook sausage patties.
3. To serve, place toast slices on individual plates. Place sausage in the circle, top with a scoop of eggs and a slice of cheese. Then place the circle of toast on top.

Yield: 4 servings

Papa Bear was in the kitchen when Brother Bear walked in, looking for a snack.

"No time for a snack, Brother," said Papa. "Why don't you wash your hands and help me make lunch for the family?"

"Can I really help?" asked Brother. "You know, Mama and Sister really like those mini pizzas we had last week. Can we make those again, Papa?"

Papa smiled. "That's just what I was thinking, Brother. If we add ice cold milk and fruit, it will be just right for lunch."

"Woo-hoo!" shouted Brother, as he headed for the sink to wash his hands.

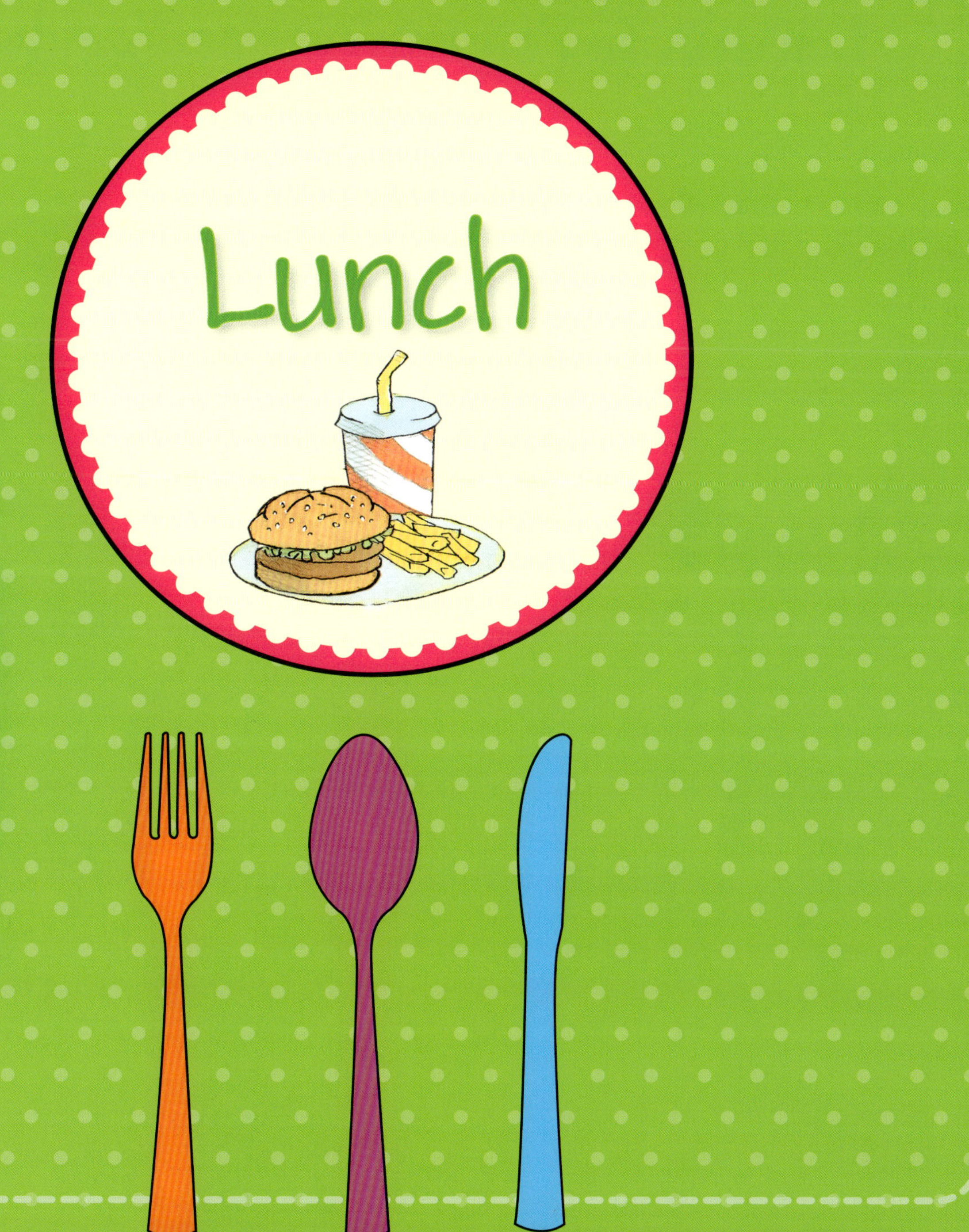
Lunch

Banana & Peanut Butter Sandwiches

What you need:

- 1 slice of bread
- 2 tablespoons peanut butter
- 2 teaspoons raisins
- 1 banana, sliced
- Honey

Directions

1. Toast bread.
2. Spread with peanut butter.
3. Sprinkle with raisins.
4. Place banana slices on top.
5. Drizzle lightly with honey.

Yield: 1 serving

Creamy Chicken Noodle Soup

What you need:

- 2 (10–3/4 oz.) cans cream of mushroom soup
- 1 (10–3/4 oz.) cans cream of chicken soup
- 2–1/2 cups water
- 1 pound cooked chicken, shredded
- 1 (9 oz.) package frozen mixed vegetables, thawed
- 1 teaspoon ground black pepper
- 1/2 teaspoon rosemary
- 1/2 teaspoon thyme
- 1/2 teaspoon celery salt
- 2 cups egg noodles

Directions

1. In a pot, pour all three cans of soup and water.
2. Whisk together until smooth. Bring to a boil.
3. Stir in chicken, vegetables, thyme, rosemary, celery salt, pepper, and dried egg noodles.
4. Cover and cook on low-medium heat for another 15–20 minutes, until chicken and vegetables are hot and the noodles are tender. Stir well.

Yield: 4–6 servings

Crustless Tuna Sandwiches

What you need:

- 1 (12 oz.) can tuna in water
- 5 celery stalks, diced
- 3–4 tablespoons mayonnaise
- Salt and pepper to taste
- 6 slices of bread
- 6 romaine lettuce leaves

Directions

1. Drain tuna and put into a bowl.
2. Chop celery into small pieces and place in bowl with tuna.
3. Add mayonnaise.
4. Mix ingredients well.
5. Cut the crust off your favorite kind of bread and spread the tuna salad onto the bread.
6. Top with a romaine lettuce leaf and fold.

Yield: 6 servings

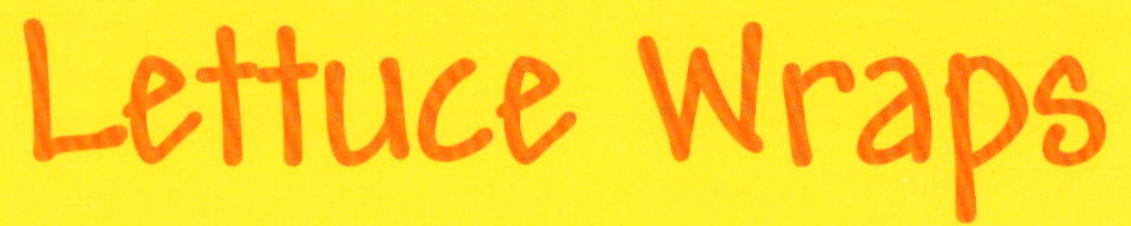

What you need:

- 1 large head romaine lettuce
- 1–1/2 cups chopped cherry tomatoes
- 1–1/2 cups chopped cucumber
- 3/4 cup nonfat plain yogurt
- 2 tablespoons chopped fresh mint
- 1 tablespoon lemon juice
- 1/2 teaspoon salt

Directions

1. Wash and dry tomatoes. Cut in half.
2. Peel cucumber and cut into bite-size pieces.
3. Combine yogurt, mint, lemon juice, and salt. Mix well.
4. Divide the tomatoes and cucumbers into 6–7 servings and place into a large lettuce leaf.
5. Pour a small portion of the yogurt mixture over each serving.
6. Fold each lettuce leaf closed.
7. You could also grill chicken or other meat to put in lettuce wraps.

Yield: 6–7 servings

Mini Pizzas

What you need:

- 6 slices French bread
- 2 tablespoons butter
- 1 cup pizza sauce
- Pizza toppings (cheese, pepperoni, ham, green peppers, mushrooms, etc.)

Directions

1. Preheat oven to 400 degrees.
2. Lightly butter the bread slices and place on a baking sheet.
3. Top each slice with desired toppings, sauce first.
4. Bake for 8–10 minutes or until cheese is melted and edges are light brown.

Yield: 3 servings

Spinach Salad

What you need:

- 1 (5 oz.) container baby spinach
- 1 cup sliced almonds
- 1 cup dried cranberries
- Poppyseed dressing

Directions

1. Place spinach into large serving bowl.
2. Top with sliced almonds and cranberries.
3. Serve the salad and then top with poppyseed dressing.

Yield: 6 servings

Shepherd's Pie

What you need:

- 1 pound ground beef
- 1/2 cup chopped onion
- 1 can cream of mushroom soup
- 1 tablespoon ketchup
- 1/8 teaspoon pepper
- 2–1/2 cups milk
- 1/4 cup butter (1/2 stick)
- 2 cups instant mashed potato flakes

Directions

1. Heat the oven to 400 degrees.
2. Cook the beef and onion until well–browned stirring often. Drain off any fat.
3. Stir in the soup, ketchup, and pepper. Spoon into a 9–inch pie plate.
4. Heat the milk and butter in a 2–quart saucep to a boil. Remove from heat. Stir in the potat flakes. (This will be stiff.) Spoon and spread over the beef mixture.
5. Bake for 20 minutes or until potatoes are lightly browned.

Yield: 4–6 servings

Sub Sandwich

What you need:

- 1 footlong sub bun
- 3 tablespoons mayonnaise
- 2 romaine lettuce leaves
- 1 tomato, sliced
- 1 green pepper, sliced
- 4 slices turkey
- 4 square slices cheese

Directions

1. Cut bread down the middle lengthwise to create space for ingredients.
2. Spread mayonnaise (or mustard) on the bread.
3. Layer the ingredients onto the bread one at a time. You can use as many ingredients as you want! Get creative with it!

Yield: 1 footlong sandwich

Try mixing mustard with honey for
a sweet and tangy sandwich spread.

Tomato & Bacon Quiche

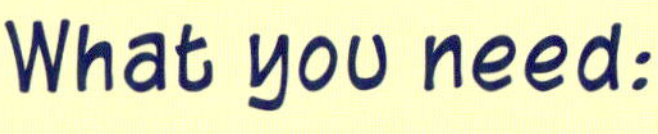

- 1 frozen deep dish pie crust
- 1 cup half-and-half
- 2 tablespoons all-purpose flour
- 2 eggs
- 1 cup shredded cheddar cheese
- 6 slices bacon, cooked, crumbled
- 3 medium plum (Roma) tomatoes, seeded, chopped
- 1/4 teaspoon salt

Directions

1. Place cookie sheet on oven rack. Heat oven to 375 degrees. Remove crust from freezer; let stand 1 minute. Prick crust with fork. Bake on cookie sheet 9–11 minutes or until very light golden brown.
2. In medium bowl, stir together half-and-half, flour, and eggs. Stir in cheese. Stir in bacon, tomatoes, and salt. Pour over crust.
3. Bake on cookie sheet 25–30 minutes longer or until knife inserted in center comes out clean. Let stand 10 minutes before serving.

Yield: 6 servings

Turkey Shaped Sandwiches

What you need:

- 9 slices of bread
- 8 tablespoons mayonnaise
- 4 slices of turkey
- 4 slices of cheese
- 1 red pepper, cut into sticks
- 1 yellow pepper, cut into sticks
- Baby carrots thinly sliced
- 8 peas

Directions

1. Cut 8 slices of bread into small squares.
2. Cut four small circles out of the last slice, to be used for the heads.
3. Spread mayonnaise on 4 pieces of bread. Arrange one slice of turkey and one slice of cheese on each sandwich. Top with the other 4 slices of bread.
4. Insert the peppers and carrots into the top of the sandwich, leaving them to stick out so they look like tail feathers.
5. Place the small circles on top of the sandwich. Place two peas for the eyes. Cut down two sticks of the yellow and red pepper and arrang[e] them onto the circles for the beak and wattle.

Yield: 4 sandwiches

Eating dinner together is an important part of the Bear family's day. No matter how busy, no matter what is going on in Bear Country, Mama and Papa want their family to share a meal and the events of their day each evening.

Mama put Honey Bear in her high chair and gave her a piece of whole wheat bread and honey as she and Papa started getting ready to make dinner together.

"Brother and Sister will be very hungry when they get home from baseball practice," said Papa.

"You're right, dear. Let's make a salad to go with the Green Noodle Lasagna," said Mama.

"And biscuits and honey too?" asked Papa.

Mama laughed. "Biscuits and honey too!" she said as she began taking the pots and pans out of the cupboard. It was going to be another delicious Bear family dinnertime.

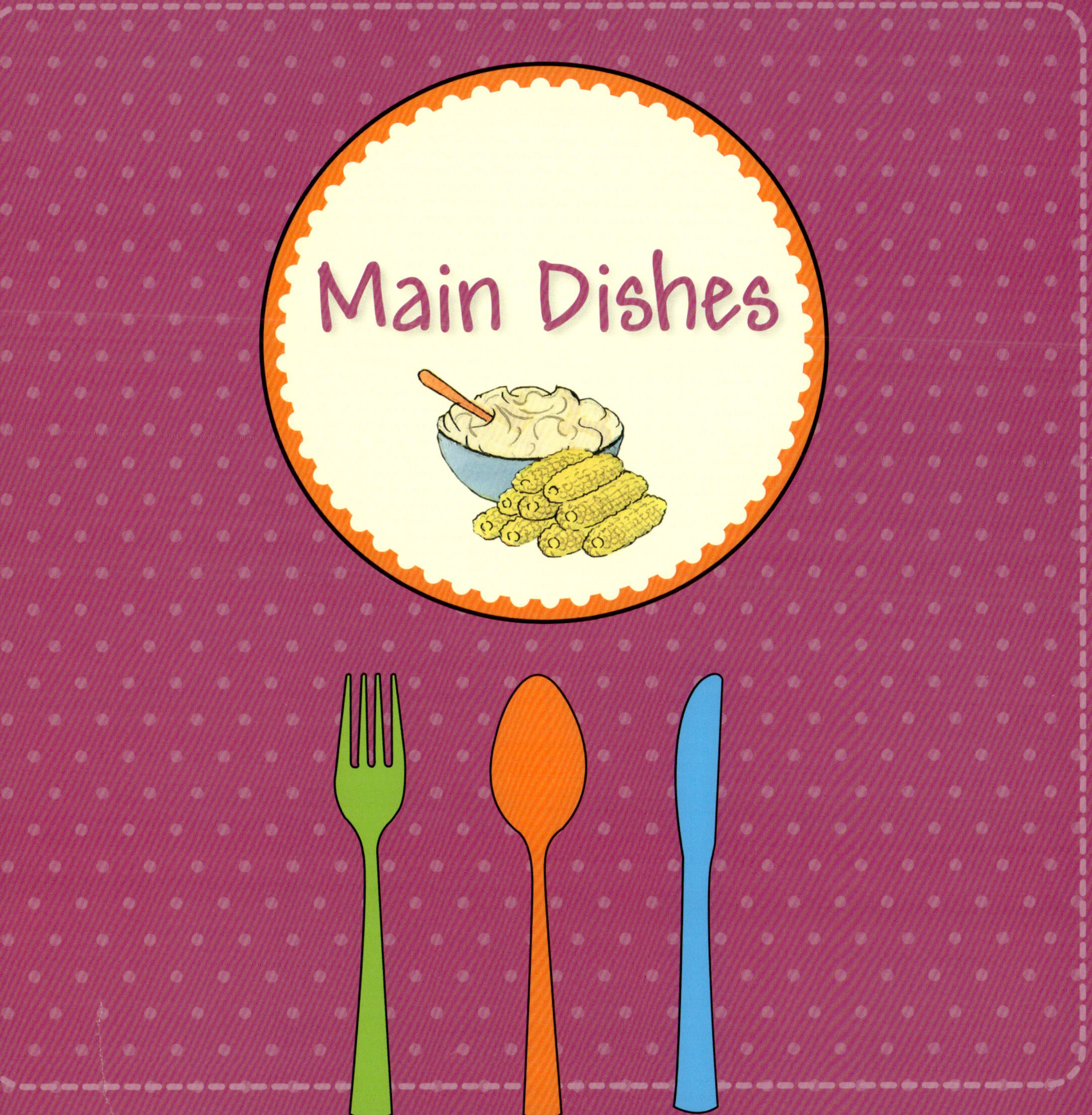
Main Dishes

What you need:

- 1 (16 oz.) package elbow macaroni
- 3 cups (24 oz.) cottage cheese
- 1/2 cup butter, cubed
- 1/2 cup all–purpose flour
- 1 teaspoon salt
- 1/2 teaspoon white pepper
- 1/4 teaspoon garlic salt
- 3 cups half–and–half
- 1 cup milk
- 4 cups shredded cheddar cheese
- 1/2 cup butter, melted
- 1 cup dry bread crumbs

Directions

1. Cook macaroni according to package directions. Meanwhile, place cottage cheese in a food processor; cover and process until smooth. Set aside.
2. In a large saucepan, melt 1/2 cup butter. Stir in the flour, salt, pepper, and garlic salt until smooth. Gradually add cream and milk. Bring to a boil; cook and stir for 2 minutes or until thickened.
3. Drain macaroni; Transfer to a large mixing bowl. Add cheddar cheese, cottage cheese, and white sauce. Stir well. Transfer to a greased 13 x 9–inch baking dish. (Dish will be full.) Combine bread crumbs and butter; sprinkle over the top.
4. Bake, uncovered, at 400 degrees for 20–25 minutes or until bubbly.

Yield: 12 servings (1 cup each)

Corn on the Cob

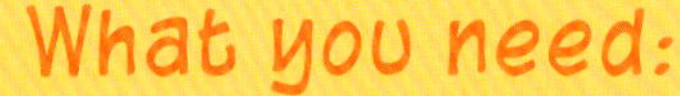

What you need:

- Fresh ears of corn, husks and silk removed
- Butter
- Salt and pepper, to taste

Directions

1. Choose a pot large enough to hold the amount of corn you want to cook. Fill the pot with water so that the water will cover the corn.
2. Cover the pot and bring the water to a boil on high heat.
3. Add the corn to the water and cover. Cook corn for 3–10 minutes, depending on how soft you want the kernels.
4. Serve with butter, salt, and pepper

Try adding some honey to your butter for a sweet kettle-corn treat.

Easy Enchiladas

What you need:

- 1 (28 oz.) can red enchilada sauce
- 12 flour tortillas
- 2 cups shredded Mexican cheese
- 1 (16 oz.) can refried beans
- 2 cups cooked, shredded beef or chicken

Directions

1. Pour a little bit of the red enchilada sauce into a 9 x 13–inch baking dish. Coat the bottom of the pan.
2. In each flour tortilla, put some refried beans, meat, and shredded cheese. Roll up and place into the baking dish, seam side down.
3. Pour remaining red enchilada sauce over the enchiladas.
4. Sprinkle remaining shredded cheese on top.
5. Cover the dish with foil and bake for 25 minutes at 350 degrees.
6. Remove the foil and bake for an additional 5 minutes.

Yield: 12 enchiladas

Green Noodle Lasagna

What you need:

- 1 package spinach lasagna noodles
- 2 cups cut–up, cooked veal or chicken
- 3/4 cup braised, sliced mushrooms (or small can)
- 2 (6 oz.) packages skim milk mozzarella cheese
- 1 (1 lb.) container of skim–milk cottage cheese
- 1 cup grated Parmesan cheese
- Salt to taste

White Sauce

- 3/4 cup margarine
- 3/4 cup flour
- 1 teaspoon salt
- 1/4 teaspoon pepper
- 4 cups skim milk
- 2 teaspoons Worcestershire sauce
- Minced or dried parsley

Directions

White sauce:

1. Melt margarine in saucepan.
2. Take saucepan off the heat and blend in flour, salt, and pepper.
3. Add milk gradually to blend in smoothly, then return to heat and cook, stirring constantly until thickened.
4. Remove from heat and stir in Worcestershire sauce and a heaping teaspoon of parsley.
5. Cook noodles according to instructions on the package.
6. In a 9 x 13–inch baking dish alternately layer noodles, veal or chicken, mushrooms, large dots of cheese, sprinkles of sliced and broken mozzarella, and sauce—ending with the sauce.
7. Sprinkle top liberally with Parmesan cheese and lightly with parsley flakes.
8. Bake in oven at 350 degrees F for 45–50 minutes.
9. Let stand for 15 minutes before cutting.

Yield: 12 servings

From the
Kitchen of
JAN
BERENSTAIN

Grilled Chicken with Carrots

What you need:

- 3 whole chicken breasts, split
- 2 tablespoons Italian seasoning
- 1 tablespoon garlic powder
- 1 pound baby carrots
- 2 teaspoons butter
- 2 tablespoons honey

GOD BLESS OUR HOME

Directions

1. Place carrots into a large pot and cover with water. Bring to a boil over high heat, then reduce heat to medium low, cover, and simmer until tender, about 15 minutes. Drain.
2. Combine Italian seasoning and garlic powder in to a bowl and use as a dry rub on the chicken breasts. Place chicken breasts on the grill and cook for 8–10 minutes or until golden brown and cooked all the way through. Turn them halfway through so they cook evenly on both sides and get the grill marks.
3. Place carrots into a serving bowl and add butter and honey. Toss to coat.

Yield: 6 servings

Meat & Potato Kabobs

What you need:

- 1 pound small red potatoes
- 1 (16 oz.) package smoked sausage
- 14 cherry tomatoes
- 14 mushrooms

Directions

1. Soak 6–8 wooden skewers in water for 30 minutes.
2. Scrub potatoes.
3. Cut potatoes in half. Cut sausage into 1/2–inch thick chunks. Cut tomatoes and mushrooms in half.
4. In large saucepan, cook potatoes in boiling, salted water for 5–10 minutes until almost tender. Drain.
5. Fry the sausage until heated through, then add mushrooms to the pan and continue cooking for 3 more minutes.
6. Assemble the kabobs on the skewers, alternating sausage, potato, mushroom, and tomato.
7. Grill or broil over medium heat for 3–4 minutes.

Yield: 6–8 servings

Chicken Quesadillas

What you need:

- 4 whole wheat tortillas
- 2 cups shredded Mexican or Cheddar cheese
- 1 cup shredded or diced cooked chicken
- Black beans, drained and rinsed
- Salsa and sour cream, if desired

Directions

1. Spray a frying pan with nonstick cooking spray. Heat on medium. Place one tortilla in the pan.
2. Top with 1/2 of the cheese and meat. Top with beans if desired. Place a second tortilla on top.
3. Cook quesadillas for 2 minutes on both sides or until cheese is melted.
4. Repeat for the second quesadilla.
5. Cut each into 4 pieces and serve with salsa and sour cream, if desired.

Yield: 2 servings

Red Beans, Sausage & Rice

What you need:

- 1/2 tablespoon canola oil
- 1 small onion, diced
- 2 celery sticks, sliced
- 1/3 cup green bell pepper, diced
- 2 garlic cloves, minced
- 1 tablespoon Creole seasoning
- 12 oz. andouille (hot and spicy) sausage
- 1 tablespoon tomato paste
- 2 tablespoons fresh parsley, chopped
- 2 cups uncooked rice
- 2 cups chicken broth
- 2 bay leaves
- 1 (15–oz.) can kidney beans, drained and rinsed

Directions

1. Heat oil in a large skillet that has a lid. Sauté onion, celery, bell pepper, garlic, and 1/2 tablespoon of Creole seasoning over medium-high heat until tender.
2. Add sausage and cook until brown. Stir in tomato paste, parsley, and rice; cook 1 minu
3. Add chicken broth, bay leaves, remaining Creole seasoning, and kidney beans. Mix we and bring to a boil over high heat.
4. Cover skillet, reduce heat to low, and cook until rice is done (about 20 minutes).
5. Remove from heat and let sit for a few minutes before serving.

Yield: 4 servings

Skillet Fried Potatoes

What you need:

- 2–3 tablespoons vegetable oil
- 1 pound frozen potato puffs
- 1/4 teaspoon garlic powder
- 1 teaspoon ground paprika
- 1/2 teaspoon salt
- 1/2 teaspoon freshly ground black pepper
- 1 slice green pepper
- Handful of steamed veggies
- 1 olive, sliced
- 2 small spoonfuls of sour cream
- 1 cherry tomato

Directions

1. Heat oil in a large, heavy, nonstick skillet or electric skillet over medium heat. Add potatoes, paprika, salt, pepper, and garlic powder.
2. Cover and cook for about 10–15 minutes, or until potatoes are just tender.
3. Uncover and increase heat to medium–high. Continue cooking for about 8–10 minutes, turning occasionally until nicely browned.
4. Steam the veggies in a little bit of water either in the microwave or in a pan on the stove.
5. Sprinkle the veggies over the crispy fried potatoes.
6. Put two dabs of sour cream on the potatoes and put two slices of olives on the sour cream, to make eyes.
7. Arrange the cherry tomato and the slice of green pepper to make a nose and mouth.

Yield: 4–6 servings

White Chicken Chili

What you need:

- 6 boneless chicken breasts
- 1 large onion, finely chopped
- 3 tablespoons olive oil
- 1 (4–oz.) can of chopped green chilies
- 1 (4–oz.) can of chopped jalapeños
- 1 tablespoon cumin
- 1 tablespoon oregano
- 1 tablespoon chili powder
- 1 tablespoon chopped garlic
- 4 (15–oz.) cans navy beans, drained
- 1 (15–oz.) can chili beans
- 4 cups of chicken broth
- 2–1/2 cups shredded Monterey Jack cheese

Directions

1. Lightly season chicken breasts with salt and pepper.
2. Roast in oven at 350 degrees for 35 minutes.
3. Let cool and chop into bite-size pieces. Set aside.
4. In a heavy pan, sauté onion in oil until transparent. Add chilies, jalapeños, and all spices and continue cooking for 5 minutes.
5. Add chicken and beans and stir well.
6. Slowly add broth.
7. After bringing mixture to boil, simmer for 1 hour.
8. Take off heat and stir in cheese until melted.
9. Serve with tortilla chips.

Yield: 6 servings

Brother, Sister, Honey Bear, and Mama and Papa too, enjoy a snack or delicious dessert now and then. So when an invitation to visit Gran and Gramps on Sunday afternoon arrived, after going to Chapel in the Woods and Sunday school, the Bear family knew they may be in for one of Gran's specialty treats!

As the Bear family rode to Gran and Gramps' after church, Brother said, "I hope Gran's baking her perfect pumpkin pie."

"I'm hoping for Cola Cake," said Mama Bear.

But as they walked up the road and got nearer to Gran and Gramps' house, Papa began sniffing the air.

"I'd know that sweet smell anywhere! Gran is baking her famous Honey Hunt Cookies!" he said.

Gramps was laughing as he walked up the lane to meet the Bears. "You are absolutely right, Son! With ice cold milk they will make the perfect end to a delicious Sunday dinner."

Dessert
&
Snacks

Applesauce

What you need:

- 3–4 large apples
- 1/4 cup water
- 1/4 cup granulated sugar
- 1/2 teaspoon cinnamon
- 1 teaspoon honey (optional)

Directions

1. Peel the apples. Remove the cores and cut into small chunks.
2. Put apple chunks in a microwave–safe bowl, add water, cover lightly with a paper towel, and microwave on high for 5 minutes.
3. Poke with a fork to see if the apples are super tender. If still firm, microwave again for 2–3 more minutes.
4. Carefully take the bowl out of the microwave. Mash the apples with a potato masher or large fork.
5. Add sugar and cinnamon and stir well.
6. Drizzle with honey and serve.

Yield: 3 cups

Banana Pops

What you need:

- 7–8 bananas
- Craft sticks
- 17.6 oz. tub of Greek yogurt
- 3–4 tablespoons honey
- Toppings of your choice (sprinkles, chocolate sprinkles, chopped nuts, and/or sweetened coconut)

Directions

1. Peel and cut bananas into halves.
2. Push craft stick into the cut side of the banana.
3. Mix honey into Greek yogurt. Taste and add more honey if desired.
4. Dip the banana into the yogurt mix. Use a rubber spatula or spoon to help cover the banana evenly with the yogurt.
5. Lay the yogurt-covered bananas on a parchment paper-lined cookie sheet.
6. Freeze for 1 hour.
7. Pour sprinkles or other topping(s) in shallow bowl(s).
8. Remove yogurt-covered bananas from freezer and roll in sprinkles or other toppings.
9. Freeze on parchment paper-lined cookie shee for another hour, then store in freezer bags.

Yield: 14–16 servings

Blue-beary Pie

What you need:

- 3/4 cup sugar
- 3 tablespoons cornstarch
- 1/8 tablespoon salt
- 1/4 cup cold water
- 5 cups fresh blueberries, divided
- 1 tablespoon butter
- 1 tablespoon lemon juice
- 1 pie crust (9–inch), baked

Directions

1. In a saucepan over medium heat, combine sugar, cornstarch, salt, and water. Mix and cook until smooth.
2. Add 3 cups blueberries and bring to a boil. Cook and stir for 2 minutes or until thickened and bubbly.
3. Remove from the heat. Add butter, lemon juice, and remaining berries; stir until butter is melted. Cool. Pour into pastry shell.
4. Refrigerate one hour. When ready to eat, top with a dollop of whipped cream and some fresh blueberries.

Yield: 8 servings

Cola Cake

What you need:

- 2 cups flour
- 2 cups sugar
- 1 stick butter
- 1 cup Coca-Cola
- 3 tablespoons cocoa powder
- 1/2 cup buttermilk
- 2 eggs
- 1 teaspoon vanilla
- 1 teaspoon baking soda
- 1/2 cup miniature marshmallows

Icing:

- 1 stick butter
- 2 tablespoons Coca–Cola
- 3 teaspoons cocoa powder
- 1 cup chopped nuts
- 1 cup powdered sugar, to taste

Directions

1. Preheat oven to 350 degrees. Grease and flour a 9 x 13–inch pan.
2. Mix flour and sugar in a large bowl.
3. In a small pot, combine butter, Coca–Cola, and cocoa powder. Heat until boiling, stirring constantly.
4. Pour hot liquid into flour and sugar; mix well.
5. In a second bowl, mix buttermilk, eggs, vanilla, and baking soda. Fold into flour mixture.
6. Stir in marshmallows, then pour into the greased and floured pan.
7. Bake for 20–30 minutes, until a toothpick comes out clean.
8. While cake is baking, prepare the icing. In a small pot, melt together butter, Coca–Cola, and cocoa powder. Pour hot mixture over powdered sugar, add nuts and mix until the sugar dissolves.
9. When the cake is done baking, pour icing over the top and sides while it's still hot. Cool and serve.

Yield: 16–20 slices

Candied Pretzels

What you need:

- 1 (12 oz.) bag chocolate chips
- 1 (12 oz.) bag caramel pieces
- 24 pretzel rods
- sprinkles and nuts (optional)

Directions

1. Melt one bag chocolate chips in the microwave. Stir until smooth.
2. Melt the caramel pieces in the microwave. Stir until smooth.
3. Dip half the pretzel rod into the chocolate. (If it starts to get thick, warm in the microwave for 8–10 seconds.)
4. Dip the coated end of the pretzel into sprinkles, nuts, shredded coconut, or other toppings. You can drizzle on caramel and white chocolate too
5. Stand up in a glass or lay on a cookie sheet (prepared with cooking spray or lined with waxed paper) until set.

Yield: 24 servings

Coconut Nest with Fruit

What you need:

- 2 large biscuits of shredded wheat or 10 small cereal pieces
- 1/3 cup shredded coconut
- 1 tablespoon brown sugar
- 2 tablespoons honey
- 1/4 cup butter, melted
- 1/4 cup vanilla yogurt
- Strawberries, grapes, blueberries

Directions

1. Crumble shredded wheat into a mixing bowl.
2. Stir in coconut and brown sugar.
3. Add honey and the melted butter and mix well.
4. Line six muffin cups with foil.
5. Use a spoon or clean hands to press mixture into the bottoms and sides of lined cups to form nests.
6. Bake at 350 degrees for 10 minutes, or until lightly browned and crisp.
7. After pan has cooled, remove nests from cups by liftin out foil and carefully peeling foil off nests.
8. Fill each nest with 1 teaspoon yogurt and several piece of fresh fruit.

Yield: 6 servings

Honey Hunt Cookies

What you need:

- 1/2 cup butter, softened
- 1/2 cup packed light brown sugar
- 1/2 cup honey
- 1 egg
- 1–1/2 cups all-purpose flour
- 1/2 teaspoon baking soda
- 1/2 teaspoon salt
- 1/2 teaspoon ground cinnamon

Directions

1. Preheat oven to 350 degrees.
2. Beat together butter, brown sugar, honey, and egg in a medium bowl until smooth and creamy. Be sure to scrape the side occasionally
3. Stir in all the remaining ingredients.
4. Drop spoonfuls of dough onto a greased or lined cookie sheet.
5. Bake about 7–10 minutes or until cookies are set and edges are light brown. The cookies wi look shiny when they are done.

Yield: 24 cookies

BEAR
CUB
FAVORITE!

Mug Brownie

What you need:

- 1/2 cup flour
- 1/4 cup brown sugar
- 2 tablespoons unsweetened cocoa powder
- Pinch of salt
- 2 tablespoons canola oil
- 2 tablespoons milk, coffee, or water

Directions

1. In a heatproof mug or ramekin, stir together the dry ingredients until no lumps remain.
2. Stir in the oil and milk until you have a thick paste.
3. Microwave on high for a minute, checking after 30 seconds (microwaves vary)—it will be done when it's springy on top but still a bit gooey—like the very best brownie.
4. Eat warm.

Yield: 1 mug brownie

Panda Cupcakes

What you need:

- 1 batch of your favorite cupcakes
- 1 (12 oz.) container whipped white frosting
- 1 tube red gel icing
- Black jellybeans
- Raisins
- Chocolate sandwich cookies
- Tic–tacs

Directions

1. Bake cupcakes as directed on package. Allow to cool.
2. Spread frosting on top of cupcakes.
3. Use 2 cookies for the ears, a black jelly bean for the nose, 2 raisins and 2 tic–tacs for the eyes. Put tic–tacs on top of the raisins with a dab of frosting. Use the red gel to make a mouth.

Yield: 12–24 cupcakes

Race Car Cookies

What you need:

- 4 fudge–covered wafer cookies
- 4 chocolate–covered caramels
- 16 round, colorful candies
- Assorted fruit snacks
- 1/2 cup chocolate frosting

Directions

1. For each car, you will need 1 cookie, 1 caramel, 4 round candies, a fruit snack, and frosting.
2. Build each car by spreading a dab of frosting on each round candy and pressing them onto the sides of the cookie as tires. Do the same with the caramel, as shown in the picture.
3. An adult can help trim the fruit snack into number shapes, stripes, and even flames at the back of each car.

Yield: 4 cookies

Grace Before Meals

Dear God,
Everything good comes from you—
family, friends, home, and food.
We thank you for these great gifts.
Bless this food we are about to eat,
And those who grew and prepared it.
Bless each of us here,
and all those we love who cannot be with us today.
We give thanks in Jesus' name,
Amen.

Sweet Facts About HONEY

The average worker bee produces about 1⁄12 teaspoon of honey in its lifetime.

For each cup of sugar in a recipe, you can substitute ¾ cup plus one tablespoon of honey.

A honeybee will visit between 50 100 flowers while out on one trip away from the hive.

Honey isn't just good to eat. It has been used for centuries to treat cuts, burns, and insect bites.

Honey is the only food produced by insects that humans eat.

Honey is sweeter than regular white table sugar.

Sticky Tips

To get honey to slide easily out of a measuring cup, use that same measuring cup for the oil first while cooking and don't wipe it out. Or spray the measuring cup with a little nonstick cooking spray before measuring the honey.

To get that last little bit of honey out of the bottle, microwave the bottle for 10 seconds, and it will slide right out.

Kitchen Measurements

8 Pinches = 1 Tablespoon

2 Tablespoons = 1/8 Cup

4 Tablespoons = 1/4 Cup

3 Teaspoons = 1 Tablespoon

5 Tablespoons, 1 Teaspoon = 1/3 Cup

 8 Tablespoons = 1/2 Cup 

 16 Tablespoons = 1 Cup 

 2 Cups = 1 Pint 

 2 Pints = 1 Quart 

 4 Cups = 1 Quart 

 4 Quarts = 1 Gallon 

So whether you eat or
drink or whatever you do,
do it all for the glory of God.

—1 Corinthians 10:31